Materials

Paper

Chris Oxlade

Heinemann
LIBRARY

www.heinemann.co.uk/library
Visit our website to find out more information about **Heinemann Library** books.

To Order:
Phone 44 (0) 1865 888066
Send a fax to 44 (0) 1865 314091
Visit the Heinemann Library Bookshop at www.heinemann.co.uk/library to browse our catalogue and order online.

First published in Great Britain by Heinemann Library, Halley Court, Jordan Hill, Oxford OX2 8EJ
a division of Reed Educational and Professional Publishing Ltd.
Heinemann is a registered trademark of Reed Educational & Professional Publishing Ltd.

OXFORD   MELBOURNE   AUCKLAND   JOHANNESBURG   BLANTYRE
GABORONE   IBADAN   PORTSMOUTH   (NH)   USA   CHICAGO

Designed by Storeybooks
Originated by Ambassador Litho Ltd.
Printed in Hong Kong / China

ISBN 0 431 12725 5 (hardback)   ISBN 0 431 12732 8 (paperback)
05 04 03 02 01   06 05 04 03 02
10 9 8 7 6 5 4 3 2   10 9 8 7 6 5 4 3 2 1

British Library Cataloguing in Publication Data
Oxlade, Chris
Paper. – (Materials)
1. Paper
I. Title
620.1'97

Acknowledgements
Corbis pp 14, /Philip Gould p.4, /Jacqui Hurst p.23, /Paul Seheult/Eye Ubiquitous p.26, /Ron Watts p.18; DIY Photo Library p.24; Elizabeth Whiting Associates p.25; Jacqui Hurst p.17; Photodisc pp.19, 20, 21, 27; Powerstock Zefa pp.11, 16, 28; Science Photo Library /Colin Cuthbert p.15, /Microfield Scientific Ltd. p12, /Tommaso Guicciardini p.13; Tudor Photography pp. 5, 6, 7, 8, 9, 10, 22.

Cover photograph: Heinemann Library.

Every effort has been made to contact copyright holders of any material reproduced in this book. Any omissions will be rectified in subsequent printings if notice is given to the Publisher.

Contents

You can find words shown in bold, **like this**, in the Glossary.

What is paper?

Paper is made in workshops and **factories**. It is not a **natural** material. This paper has just been made. It is stored on rolls, ready to be made into newspapers.

Paper has many uses. Most paper is made
into newspapers, books and magazines. It
is also used for bags and wrapping. All the
things in this picture are made from paper.

Strong and weak

Paper is easy to scrunch up into a ball.
It is also easy to tear into pieces. A
sheet of paper is quite strong, though, if
you try to stretch it or pull it apart.

A sheet of paper can be made much stiffer by folding it. This girl is using a paper fan to keep cool. The fan is stiff because of the folds in the paper.

Paper and card

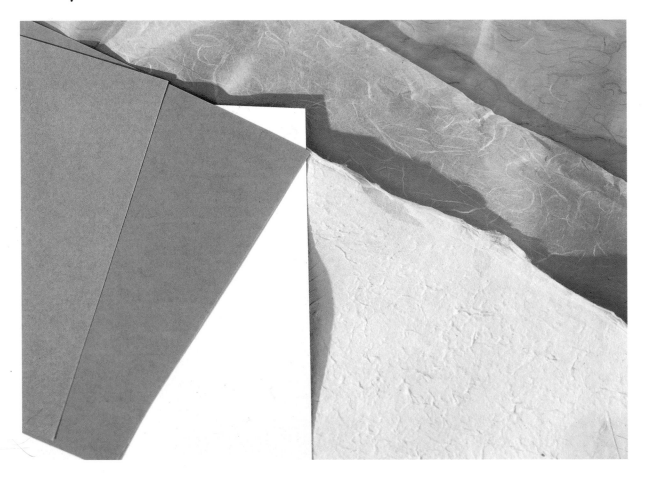

There are many different kinds of paper. The paper in this book has a smooth, shiny **surface**. Other types of paper have a rough surface. Some are coloured with dyes.

Card is thick, stiff paper, normally with a smooth surface. It comes in different thicknesses. **Cardboard** is very thick and stiff. One kind has a wavy sheet of card in the centre. This makes it even stiffer.

Wet and dry

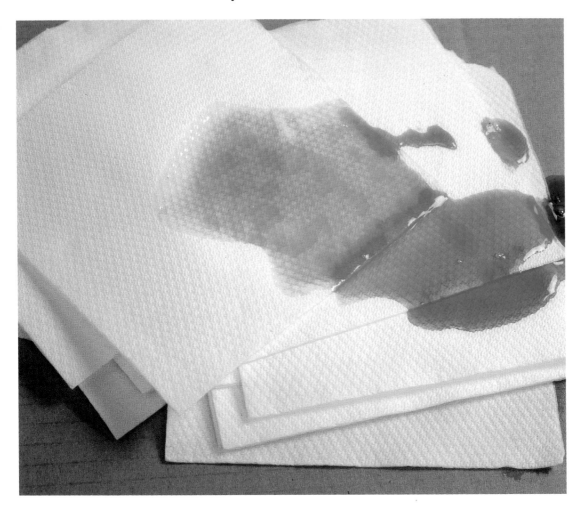

Paper towels and handkerchiefs are made of paper that soaks up **liquid** very well. The liquid flows into tiny spaces inside the paper.

Paper containers for liquids are made from paper that does not soak up water at all. The paper is covered with a thin layer of **wax** or plastic.
This stops the water going through the paper.

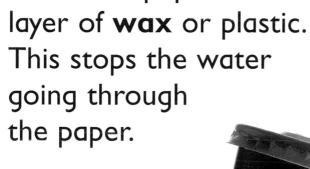

Making paper

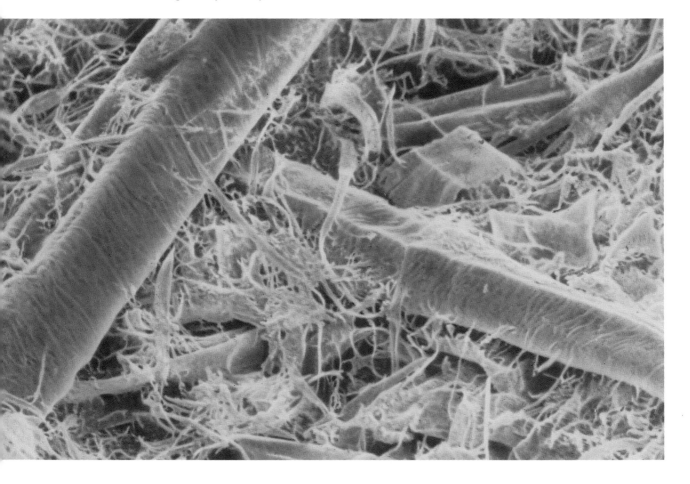

Paper is made from tiny **fibres** that come from plants. You can see the fibres when you tear paper. Most fibres used for making paper come from wood. The wood comes from trees.

Paper is made at a **factory** called a **paper mill**. Wood is mixed with water and **chemicals**. Then it is mashed up by machines to make wood **pulp**. It looks like a thick paste.

Drying and rolling

The runny wood **pulp** is poured onto a wire mesh, which works like a large, flat sieve. The mesh catches the woody fibres but lets the water drain away. This makes a layer of wet paper.

The wet paper is taken off the mesh. Then the rest of the water is squeezed out by heavy rollers and the paper is dried. The finished paper is put on big rolls, or it is cut into sheets.

Writing and painting

Paper for writing has a smooth **surface**.
The surface is covered in **chemicals**.
They stop the ink from a pen soaking
into the paper and becoming blotchy.

This painting is being done on thick
paper that soaks up watery paints. The
paper is called water-colour paper. It will
dry out when the painting is finished.

Printing on paper

Most paper is used for **printing**. It is made into newspapers, books and magazines. This paper is going through a newspaper **press**.

Bank notes are printed on paper that has strong **fibres** in it. This makes the paper difficult to tear. The notes last for more than a year before they wear out.

Paper packaging

Many packaging materials are made
from paper. Gift wrapping paper often
has patterns printed on it. Paper bags
are made by folding and gluing paper.

Cardboard is used to make strong boxes. The boxes protect things inside. A flat piece of cardboard is folded to make a box shape. The edges of the cardboard are joined with glue or metal **staples**.

Paper objects

Many objects are made by cutting, folding and gluing paper. These boxes and aeroplanes are made from thin card and paper.

This plate is made from a material called papier mâché. You make papier mâché by mashing up wet paper and glue. It goes very hard when it dries.

Paper in homes

The walls of this home are being decorated with wallpaper with a raised pattern on it. The wallpaper is thick and heavy. It is being pasted to the walls.

In some Japanese homes, screens made of wood and paper are used instead of walls between rooms. Sheets of paper are glued onto wooden frames to make screens and sliding doors.

Recycling paper

Millions of trees are cut down every day to make paper. **Paper mills** use lots of electricity. Trees and electricity can be saved by using paper again. This is called recycling.

Paper sent for recycling is mashed up to make wood **pulp**. Ink from **printing** is removed from the pulp with **chemicals**. Most recycled paper is used to make newspapers and **cardboard**.

Fact file

Most paper is made in **factories**. It is not a **natural** material.

Paper is easy to scrunch into a ball and tear.

Paper is hard to stretch and pull apart.

Paper can be made stiffer by folding it.

Paper can be smooth or rough. It can be white or coloured.

Card is thicker and stiffer than paper.

Some kinds of paper are waterproof. Some kinds soak up water.

Paper does not let electricity or heat flow through it.

Paper burns when it is heated.

Paper is not attracted by **magnets**.

Would you believe it?

Paper for newspapers comes on huge rolls as tall as a grown-up person and as heavy as a family car. If a roll was unrolled, it would be about 15 kilometres long. It would take a grown-up three hours to walk that far!

Glossary

card thick, stiff paper with a smooth surface

cardboard very stiff, thick material made from layers of card and paper

chemicals special materials that are used in factories and homes to do jobs like cleaning and protecting

factory place where things are made using machines

fibre thin thread or tiny piece of a material. Paper fibres come from the trees or plants the paper is made from.

liquid substance that flows, such as water and oil

magnet object that attracts iron or steel

natural comes from plants, animals or rocks in the earth

paper mill factory where paper is made

press machine that prints inks onto paper

printing making patterns, words or pictures on paper by pressing ink onto the paper

pulp mixture of wood and water that has been mashed together

staple piece of metal wire that sticks through sheets of paper, card or cardboard, joining them

surface top or outside of an object

wax material that feels smooth and oily and does not let water through. Candles are made of wax.

More books to read

Materials: Wood
Chris Oxlade
Heinemann Library, 2001

What are. . . ? Forests
A. Owen and M. Ashwell
Heinemann Library, 1998

Step-by-Step: Papermaking
David Watson
Heinemann Library, 2000

I Can Help Recycle Rubbish
Franklin Watts

Science Explorers: Paper
A & C Black, 1999

Index